Super Awesome Jokes

For 6-12 Year Old Kids

Laugh Till You Cry!!

Copyright © 2019
All rights reserved.

No part of this publication may be reproduced, distributed or transmitted in any form or by any means including photocopying, recording or other electronic or mechanical methods without prior permission of the publisher.

ISBN: 9781710605532

Get Ready!

Hey jokester! Stop looking around, yes you! This silly joke book is loaded with really funny jokes just for you. No matter how serious you are, there is something here to crack you up!

Have fun springing some of these silly question and answer jokes on your family and friends.

You will be like a star comedian in no time. Have fun!

Start Laughing!

Why can't leopards play hide and seek?

They are always spotted!

• •

What did the kitten eat for breakfast?

Mice-krispies!

Why did the chicken wear a shellsuit?

It's an egg!

• •

Why was the chicken awarded for employee of the year?

He worked around the cluck!

What do you call a dog that is sweating?

A hot-dog!

• • • • • • • • • • • • • • • • • •

Why did the fish have three eyes?

It's a fiiish!

What did the daddy chimney say to the baby chimney?

You are too young to smoke!

• •

What do you call a baby bee?

A little hum-bug!

Why didn't the skeleton go to the party?

He had no body to go with him.

• • • • • • • • • • • • • • • • • • •

What day do chickens hate most?

Fry-days!

Where did the hamburger go dancing?

At a meat-ball!

• • • • • • • • • • • • • • • • • • •

How can you make a fire with two sticks?

Make sure one is a match!

What did the belt do to go to jail?

It held up a pair of pants.

• • • • • • • • • • • • • • • • • •

How do hair stylists work faster?

They take short cuts!

What does a boxer like to drink?

Punch!

• • • • • • • • • • • • • • •

How do you get a tissue to start dancing?

You put a little boogie into it!

Where do cows go when they want to have fun?

The moo-vies!

• • • • • • • • • • • • • • • • • • • •

Why couldn't the pony sing in the choir?

Because she was a little hoarse!

What makes the fish so smart?

They live in schools.

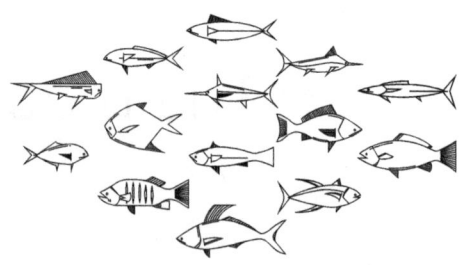

••••••••••••••••••••

Where does the rooster like to eat?

At a rooster-ant!

What did the male firefly say to the female one?

You glow, girl!

● ● ● ● ● ● ● ● ● ● ● ● ● ● ● ● ● ● ● ●

How can you help a lemon?

Make it some lemonade.

Why can't you tell a joke while you're standing on ice?

Because it might crack up!

• • • • • • • • • • • • • • • • • •

What flying creature is smarter than a talking parrot?

A spelling bee.

What is big, blue and eats rocks?

A Big Blue Rock Eater!

• • • • • • • • • • • • • • • • • •

What do you call a toothless bear ?

A gummy bear!

What stays in a corner but travels around the world?

A post stamp!

• •

What has no hands or feet but touches every continent?

The ocean.

Where did the student learn to make banana splits?

At sundae school!

• •

What does a clock do when it is hungry?

It goes back 4 seconds!

Why did the banana go to the doctor?

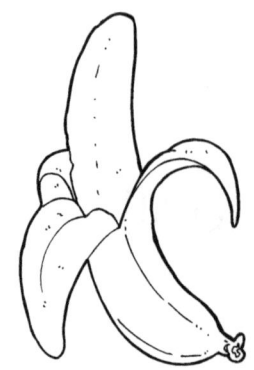

He was peeling really bad.

● ● ● ● ● ● ● ● ● ● ● ● ● ● ●

Where do you put barking dogs?

In a barking lot.

Why was the math book feeling sad?

Because it had so many problems.

• • • • • • • • • • • • • • • • • • • •

Who can shave six times a day, but still have a hair on his head?

A barber!

Why did the girl eat her homework?

Because her teacher told her it was a piece of cake!

• • • • • • • • • • • • • • • •

What kind of shoes do frogs like to wear?

Open toad.

What gets wetter the more it dries?

A towel!

● ● ● ● ● ● ● ● ● ● ● ● ● ● ● ● ● ● ● ●

Why did the dog do his school work so well?

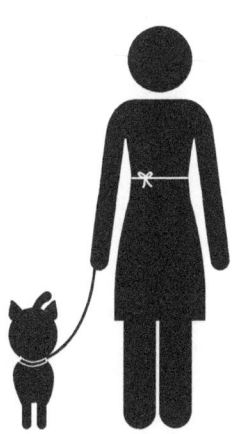

Because he was the teacher's pet!

What has to be broken before you can use it?

An egg.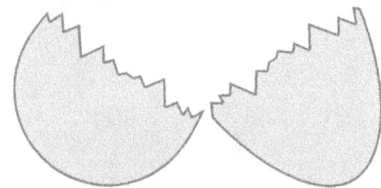

• • • • • • • • • • • • • • • • • • •

What goes up, but never comes down?

Your age.

Where do horses live?

In neigh-borhoods!

How can a girl go eight days without sleep?

She only sleeps at night!

What has keys but can't open any door?

A piano.

• • • • • • • • • • • • • • • • • • •

What is mostly green or blue, has four wheels and flies?

A garbage truck.

Which subject did the snake like most?

Hiss-tory.

Why did the sun go to school?

To get brighter!

What gets sharper the more you use it?

Your brain!

● ●

How do you cut a wave in half?

Use a sea saw.

What is full of holes but can still hold water?

A sponge.

Why did the blind man eat so many lobsters?

It's a see-food!

What do roosters do for fun?

They Doodle-doo!

• • • • • • • • • • • • • • • •

Why didn't the little girl wave at the lady?

She had a micro-wave!

What would you call a cheese that isn't yours?

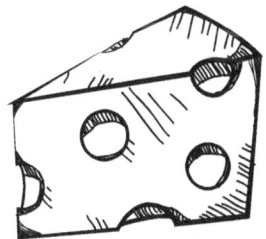

Nacho cheese!

• • • • • • • • • • • • • • • • • • •

What would you call a bull that is sleeping?

A bull-dozer.

Which planet likes to sing music?

Neptune!

• •

What did the little elf learn in school?

The elf-phabet!

Why did the melon jump into the sea?

It wanted to be a watermelon.

• • • • • • • • • • • • • • • • • • • •

Why did the boy put his glass of milk on a trampoline?

He wanted a milk-shake!

Why was it so hot at the basketball game?

All the fans left!

• •

What do you call a cow that has no legs?

Ground beef!

What do you call a silly man with a broken pencil?

 Pointless!

• • • • • • • • • • • • • • • • • • • •

How did the boy know that the ghost was lying?

He could see right through him!

Why was the girl sitting on her clock?

Because she wanted to be on time.

• • • • • • • • • • • • • • • • •

Why did the alligator want to wear a vest?

Because he wanted to be an investigator!

How many tickles can make a squid laugh?

Ten-tickles!

• • • • • • • • • • • • • • • • • • • •

Why didn't the turkey want more food?

Because he was stuffed!

What makes the moon heavy?

A full moon!

• •

What did the table say to the chair?

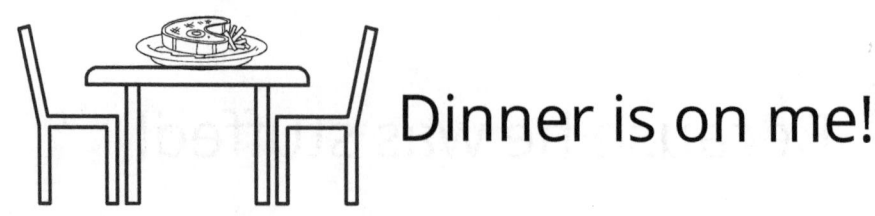 Dinner is on me!

How did the astronaut get her baby to stop crying?

She rocket!

• • • • • • • • • • • • • • • • • • • •

What did the girl use to fix the smashed tomato?

Tomato paste!

What creature is always at a cricket game?

A bat!

• •

Why was the broom late for school?

 It over-swept!

How did the science teacher freshen her breath?

She eats experi-mints!

What kind of gift did the patient give to the dentist?

A plaque!

Where do bees go after they get married?

On a honeymoon!

• • • • • • • • • • • • • • • • • • • •

What did the frog order at Burger King?

French Flies and a Croaka Cola!

Why didn't the carpenter hammer the nail?

It's a finger-nail!

• • • • • • • • • • • • • • • • • • •

Why did the photo go to jail?

It was framed.

What dinosaur is the smartest of them all?

The thesaurus!

• •

What time does most astronauts eat?

At launch time!

Why did the plant go to see the dentist?

It wanted a root canal!

How did the lawyer introduce his new girlfriend?

Meet Sue!

Why did the computer visit the doctor?

It had a virus!

● ● ● ● ● ● ● ● ● ● ● ● ● ● ● ● ● ● ●

Why did the lady put her cheque in the freezer?

She wanted to get cold, hard cash.

Why did the little girl take a ruler to bed?

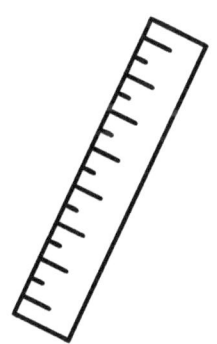

To see how long she slept!

• •

What is the name of a man lying on your doorstep?

Matt!

What did the spider's bride wear to the wedding?

A beautiful webbing dress!

• •

Why did the strawberry cry so much?

It found itself in a jam!

How did the farmer fix the broken pumpkins?

With a pumpkin patch!

• • • • • • • • • • • • • • • • • • • •

Why could the dog tell the time?

He's a watchdog!

Where did the students plant the flowers?

In the kindergarden!

• •

Why couldn't the bee make up his mind?

He's a maybe!

How do they serve smart hotdogs?

 With honor rolls!

• • • • • • • • • • • • • • • • • •

Why did the witch kiss the bee?

He's a spelling bee!

What did the sea monster have for lunch?

Fish and Ships!

• •

Why was the flashlight crying?

The batteries died!

What do you call a key that can open any door?

A don-key!

• • • • • • • • • • • • • • • • • •

Why didn't the apple win the race?

It ran out of juice!

Why does a fish always know its weight?

It has scales.

• • • • • • • • • • • • • • • • • • • •

Which creature is the helper of the sea?

A mermaid!

What do students get when they graduate from diving school?

They get a deep-loma.

• •

Why couldn't the little girl watch the pirate movie?

It was rated ARRRR!

What sea animal likes to play music?

The tune-a fish!

● ● ● ● ● ● ● ● ● ● ● ● ● ● ● ● ● ● ● ●

Why was the mountain so funny?

It's hill-arious.

Why do bananas wear sunscreen to the beach?

They might peel!

•••••••••••••••••••

What clothes did the reporter wear to work?

News briefs!

Why did the strawberry take the short cut?

To escape the traffic jam!

• •

What do fashion toads like to wear?

Jumpsuits!

Why did the man get fired from the apple juice factory?

 He couldn't concentrate!

Where did the baby ape go to sleep?

In an apri-cot!

Why did the ducks cross the playground?

To get over to the other side!

• • • • • • • • • • • • • • • • • • •

Why did the mushroom go to the disco?

He's a fun guy!

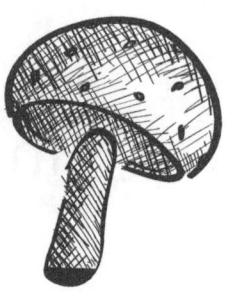

Why did the cow eat the lawn grass?

He's a lawn moo-er!

Where did the horse go after he got hurt?

To the horse-pital!

Which aunt did the little penguin love most?

Aunt Artica!

• • • • • • • • • • • • • • • • • • • •

Why is the tree better than a dog?

It has more barks!

Why did the cow eat the lawn grass?

He's a lawn moo-er!

• • • • • • • • • • • • • • • • • • • •

Where did the horse go after he got hurt?

To the horse-pital!

Which aunt did the little penguin love most?

Aunt Artica!

• •

Why is the tree better than a dog?

It has more barks!

How did the telephones get engaged?

They gave each other a ring!

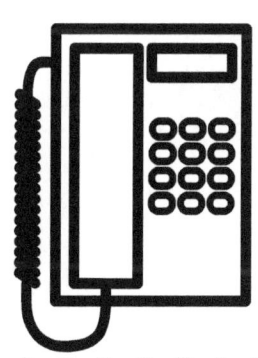

Which princess always worry about everything?

The warrior princess!

CPSIA information can be obtained
at www.ICGtesting.com
Printed in the USA
BVHW041939060420
577002BV00011B/576